Tom Greening's poetry takes on the phenomenon and complexity of aging and of being an elder with uncanny depth, wit and his trademark existential humor–befitting his fifty-year career as an existential psychotherapist. Doing away with any lightness and political correctness, these poems will not only make you smile but they will help you face a topic most of us would rather not contemplate: our mortality.

Nader Shabahangi, PhD
President, Existential-Humanistic Institute
CEO, AGeSong & Eldercare Provider

Tom Greening deals creatively with life review, fear of dying, dementia, loss, and the comforts possible in older age. He accomplishes all this with his persistent wit, unique rhyme schemes, and novel imagery. With its honesty, candor, and humor, this book deserves to be read widely.

Carol Barrett, PhD
Professor, Union Institute and University
Author, *Calling in the Bones*

I0154321

Poems For and About Elders
Revised & Expanded Edition

By Tom Greening

University
PROFESSORS PRESS

Colorado Springs, CO
www.universityprofessorspress.com

Poetry, Healing, and Growth Series

Poetry is an ancient healing art used across cultures for thousands of years. In the Poetry, Healing, and Growth book series, the healing and growth-facilitating nature of poetry is explored in depth through books of poetry and scholarship, as well as through practical guides on how to use poetry in the service of healing and growth. Poetry written with an intention to transform suffering into an artistic encounter is often different in process and style from poetry written for art's sake. This series offers engagement with the poetic greats and literary approaches to poetry while also embracing the beauty of fresh, poetic starts and encouraging readers to embark upon their own journey with poetry. Whether you are an advanced poet, avid consumer, or novice to poetry, we are confident you will find something to inspire your thinking on your personal path toward healing and growth.

Series Editors,
Carol Barrett, PhD; Steve Fehl, PsyD; Nathaniel Granger, Jr, PsyD; Tom Greening, PhD; and Louis Hoffman, PhD

Poetry, Healing, and Growth Series

Stay Awhile: Poetic Narratives on Multiculturalism and Diversity
Louis Hoffman & Nathaniel Granger, Jr. (Eds.)

Capturing Shadows: Poetic Encounters Along the Path of Grief and Loss
Louis Hoffman & Michael Moats (Eds.)

Journey of the Wounded Soul: Poetic Companions for Spiritual Struggles
Louis Hoffman & Steve Fehl (Eds.)

Our Last Walk: Using Poetry for Grieving and Remembering Our Pets
Louis Hoffman, Michael Moats, and Tom Greening (Eds.)

Poems For and About Elders (Revised & Expanded Edition)
Tom Greening

Contents

Acknowledgements

I thank the many people who supported and helped make this book possible, and all those who have encouraged my poetry writing through the years. In particular, I wish to thank Edlers Academy Press, who published the first edition of this book as well as this update, published by University Professors Press. I also thank Nader Shabahangi, who consistently encouraged my writing of *Poems For and About Elders*. Sally Gelardin and Mary Williams also provided much support and encouragement. Finally, I want to thank University Professors Press and the editors of the Poetry, Healing, and Growth Series for publishing this new volume and including it in that series.

Introduction

Tom Greening speaks from his heart, honestly sharing how he feels in his later years. Artfully employing both grace and humor, he shares his fears, regrets, resolutions, and memories. Tom practices what he preaches. Having practiced client-centered, psychodynamic existential–humanistic psychotherapy for 47 years, he composes fresh, down-to-earth, free, sometimes rhyming, verse that always challenges us through its depth and wit.

The poet has an impressive list of academic achievements: Saybrook University faculty member, Clinical Professor of Psychology at the University of California, Los Angeles, and Distinguished Adjunct Professor at Pepperdine University's Graduate School of Education and Psychology; Diplomat in Clinical Psychology, American Board of Professional Psychology; Fellow of four divisions of the American Psychological Association; and Editor, and more recently, International Editor of the *Journal of Humanistic Psychology*, from 1971 through the present.

Most impressive about Tom is not his achievements, but rather his gentle way of "being with," rather than" talking down" or "playing up" to others, both in his verse and direct contact. In whatever he does (private practice, poetry, prose, teaching), Tom's goal is "to help people empower themselves in the face of external and internal forces that threaten to determine their choices and reduce their freedom and creativity."

I met Tom through the Pacific Institute, a nonprofit educational organization that views elders as wisdom keepers and valuable social contributors irrespective of their physical and mental state. He was steady sitting in the front lobby of an AgeSong elder community in San Francisco where Pacific Institute's "Gerowellness" pre- and post-doctoral students and therapists in training applied their learning with the elders. As they built relationships with elders, the students learned from Tom that elders are their "teachers," rather than their "clients," thus leveling the playing field between them.

At our meeting in the elder community's lobby, Tom mentioned to me that he was writing a little book of poetry. The book kept growing. A year later, Elders Academy Press proudly published the poignant verse of a scholar and poet who gives us a personal glimpse into what it means to be a human being and an elder.

Now in its second edition, *Poems for and About Elders* expands upon Tom's advancing later life reflections. Readers are privileged to the inside story of how Tom feels on a daily basis to be transitioning away from an academic existence to descriptions of more immediate experiences. He guides the way by providing a blueprint to where most of us are heading, thereby lessoning our fears of the future.

Thanks, Tom, for trailblazing into the unknown forest of our later years.

Dr. Sally Gelardin

Poems

An Elder's Resolution

Just recently a blunt friend told
me that some day I may grow old.
At first I thought he spoke in jest,
and then perceived it was a test
to see if existentially
I could face this reality.
I will not do so, now or ever,
and have resolved that I'll endeavor
to stay alive and never falter,
and be the first immortal elder.

Life Goes By

There is a lot that I regret,
and even more that I forget.
It seems my life has hurried by—
I've often had to say "goodbye"
to cats and dogs, to lovers, friends—
each phase of life begins...then ends.
My spirits rise, then sometimes fall.
As years go by I've clutched at all—
the good, the bad, the in-between,
but now when I survey the scene
I'll happily confide in you:
my life has been a dream come true.

Your Desk Drawer

Fifteen years after you died
I decide it is finally time
to clean out your desk drawer.
Old pens, a single earring, a high school medal,
antiquated computer disks,
a dried out ink pad,
keys to unknown locks,
some hardened gunk
that I try in vain to scrape out,
and a Mother's Day card from the daughter
who now has three kids of her own.
I give up.
The drawer is clean enough
and ready for more stuff
that someone else will have to sort.
It's the same with memories—
Some are worth keeping,
some are easily cleaned out,
and some unwanted ones
stay stubbornly stuck.

Rescue

A search for depth—that was my goal.
Instead, my boat stuck on a shoal.
I thrashed about, but got more stuck,
surrounded by seaweed and muck.
The hours passed, the sun grew hot,
I swore at God for my sad lot.
A dolphin swimming slowly by
heard my indignant, foul-mouthed cry.
"Please hold your tongue and I will help,"
and then he freed me from the kelp.
If you get stuck here's what to do:
pray some wise fish will rescue you.

Mr. Draper's Photos

He has no memory,
only a drawer full
of disorganized photos.
Who are these people?
Parents, lovers, comrades, children?
That old house looks like Ireland.
Photos of three dogs—
a black poodle, a golden retriever,
and a husky lab...
probably all dead now.
And here is a CD of great arias
sung in languages neither of us understands.
Although graying,
Mr. Draper is younger than I am...
the erratic unfairness of fate
and our fragile brains.
He no longer remembers his dogs,
but smiles when I show him
a photo of mine.

A Consoling Thought

I tried to become virtuous
but found it much too arduous,
thus sadly I have realized
I may not end up canonized.
While lesser mortals far excel
me as I slowly sink toward hell,
I gripe and endlessly protest
and seldom give poor God a rest.
But here's a thought to ease my mind:
I'm sure good friends in hell I'll find.

Sirens

The sirens argue with silence--
Something bad is going on.
I don't want to know about it--
Let the "first responders" respond.
Unless something is happening to me--
Then I want the whole world alerted.
But the world will remain indifferent,
So I must add my voice to the sirens.
And now dogs are howling.
Will silence ever bless us again
so I can sleep through life?

Stoic

It has not eased my stress at all
to bang my head against the wall.
The wall just stands there, stolid, still--
it does not care and never will.
The same, I fear, is true of you--
no matter what I say or do
Just like the wall, you do not care
and will not sooth my dark despair.
So I'll give up and be a stoic,
And some will think I am heroic.

Homeless

And even some of us who live in fine houses
are homeless, starving, cold,
wandering the bleak streets of our minds,
hoping for the kindness of strangers
and our own kin,
or at least safety from their abuse.
"Make me a pallet on the floor," sang John Hurt,
and I'll settle for that
if he'll just sing me to sleep every night,
even those nights when we both know
there is no sleep for the haunted.

Dale's Dog

Dale's little dog is named Bambi,
but he's no baby deer.
He is himself, a charming mix,
with smooth tan fur
and perky ears,
and eyes that take you in
and win you over.
He does a good job
of entertaining and guarding Dale,
but allows me to pet him.
I'm about as old as Dale,
and my dog Ralph is failing,
so I suspect it is likely
that Bambi will outlive all three of us
and charm our survivors,
until those bright eyes darken
and he joins us
for a walk in the clouds.

To a Surgeon

Somewhere a surgeon is polishing his skills
preparing for the day
when he will cut me open
to fix something wrong
with my aging body.
I hope he is getting good at his craft
because I am counting on him
to sustain my immortality
for a reasonable fee.
Is that too much to ask?

Caring

More people I care about
are dead than alive,
and my caring does few of them much good.
Resurrection of the dead is not an option,
and caring for the living drains
my limited capacity for humanness.
I do not want to fake it,
so I struggle along as best I can
with token gestures, faltering efforts,
and occasional breakthroughs
of what may be
actual love.

Cancer Free

Those biopsies are not for me.
I much prefer my fantasy
that I'll remain quite cancer free
and live until I'm ninety-three,
and then I'll very gracefully
ascend to immortality
beyond the reach of all diseases
and sail away on heaven's breezes.
My fantasy suits me just fine—
Rejoice! I'll be declared divine!

Senile Synapses

I have a problem that's unique:
my synapses are old and squeak.
I've lubricated them with grease
but their damn squeaking will not cease.
This makes me feel conspicuous
and I get mean and querulous.
If this keeps up I have no doubt
my febrile brain will soon burn out.
I strongly wish you would advise
me how to dodge such a demise.

Hospital Waiting Room

Every day these people do their best
to face life, but it is hard for them.
The years, gravity, their bodies,
are pulling them down
and they are perplexed,
wondering what to do.
More vitamins, exercise, a change
of diet, of doctor, perhaps
a new mattress or TV?
Their grown children visit, but seldom,
being busy themselves with life,
or what passes for it.

My Mind

My mind's not what it used to be
when it performed so brilliantly.
Too often now it sputters, stalls,
behavior that annoys and galls
me so I sometimes pray
I'll wake up on a brighter day
and it will just have gone away
and I am free, lighthearted, gay,
a man who can enjoy his life
without annoying mental strife.

Exercise?

Alas, I'm lazy, fat and phobic
about all exercise aerobic.
The thought of it just makes me frown
and drives me quickly to lie down.
My friends are always warning that
I'll pay a price for being fat
and that it is a horrid sin
to veer from striving to be thin,
but while they for svelte bodies quest
I much prefer to gorge and rest.

It's Not Your Fault

When life's a struggle and no longer fun,
when you regret too much of what you've done,
it's time to hide out, disappear and cower,
and at the world malevolently glower.
It's not your fault your trip turned out so badly–
your enemies conspired against you madly.
What could you do to fight such evil forces
that caused those infidelities, divorces?
Trust in the end you're sure to be redeemed–
You're not as evil as you've sometimes seemed.

Don't Tell My Friends

I like to claim I'm aging well
but here's the truth that I don't tell:
I drift through life somnambulant,
pretending I am competent,
indulging in the fantasy
that I have reached maturity.
I shuffle, wobble, stagger, creep,
and mostly I am half asleep.
Don't tell my friends, who think I'm wise,
and would not welcome this surprise.

My Ruse

I strive and struggle to maintain
my ruse that I am not insane.
It's true I've got a messed up brain
but I have managed to sustain
a regal stance of confidence,
a lofty air of innocence.
Give me a stage on which to prance,
where I can do my fancy dance.
Beguiling fools–that is my whim–
until my bright façade grows dim.

Death Played a Trick

Death played a trick on me.
It pretended to be closing in on my friend,
dragged him down into senility,
then shifted and took his wife,
who I was sure would outlive all of us.
Death should not be so erratic.
We have a hard enough time facing it
without such capricious surprises.
Now I wait again, suspicious,
fearful that it might turn on me.

I Plan to See

I want to make it very clear:
I'm not a king, my name's not Lear.
I have two daughters, but I'm glad
they are not scheming 'gainst their dad.
They love me lots and do their best
to see that I stay well and rest.
I also have a dog who cares
and fends off tigers, wolves, and bears.
With all this help I plan to see
if I'll transcend mortality.

Iatrogenic Ills

Beware of ills iatrogenic.
They'll make you crazy and frenetic.
I know because one day last year
I found myself in dreadful fear
of what my doctor thought of me,
and fretted, quaked quite frantically.
I sensed that he'd begun to see
me lost to some dark lunacy.
The problem was, his view was right–
from sanity I've taken flight.

Senile?

An insight just went dashing by
and as it fled I made a try
to catch it, but it sped away,
thus leaving me with naught to say.
Whenever you're blessed by a thought
quick, grab it lest it come to naught.
In desperation now I pray
to save my insights of today.
Tomorrow looms, I'm unprepared,
and by my senile slippage scared.

I've Just Begun

I worked hard at eighty-five,
glad to be still strong, alive.
Now I've reached age eighty-six
still enjoying my old tricks.
Does this life go on forever?
That is surely my endeavor.
Why stop now? I've just begun
and I've learned to make it fun.
But save a spot for me in heaven
in case I quit at eighty-seven.

Snail and I

The stupid snail climbs up the sunbaked wall
thus showing that he has no brains, just gall.
Soon he is cooked inside his roasting shell
and on his way to foolish creatures' hell.
I'm glad to say that I am no such fool
and have the sense to stay where it is cool,
although some nasty critics dare to claim
the snail and I in some ways are the same.
We both have shells, though mine is hard to see,
and both can act quite self-destructively.

If There's Still Time

When I review my life I am aghast.
So little that I've done is going to last.
My days were often "full of sound and fury,"
my nights consumed by sleeplessness and worry.
Accomplishments? They faded long ago.
Their residue? I cannot claim to know.
So on I sail and hope the wind stays fair.
Perhaps someday I will real living dare.
If there's still time I'd like to see if I
have guts enough to give it one more try.

Reasons to Exist

Quite stubbornly I will persist
in seeking reasons to exist.
I know that I must age and die,
but now I'm feeling young and spry,
and while I live I'll wonder why
some day we all must say goodbye.
I need a good survival plan–
I'll make one up as best I can–
and when at last I disappear
you'll still be glad that I was here.

Accept Death?

Accept that someday we all die?
I am reluctant but will try.
I do not mind I'll soon be dead–
it is the dying that I dread.
It seems to me a dreadful waste,
not something one should do in haste.
Instead, I've made another plan
in hopes that I will be a man
who conquers death quite cleverly
and lives for an eternity.
Do I have this ability?
May I suggest you wait and see?

Don't Look Too Close

As I descend into confusion
I'm comforted by the delusion
that I can manage to sustain
the fiction that I'm really sane.
Don't look too close at what I do–
my acts of sanity are few.
Observers note with much alarm
I've clearly lost my former charm.
Yet for a while I still will try
to pass as just a quirky guy.

Mortal Dogs

Ralph's predecessors had died off.
Years ago I had lain on the kitchen floor with Damian
explaining, asking permission,
to put him to sleep.
Anthropomorphism is often a refuge of sentimentalists,
but he seemed to understand
even if I didn't.
His successor, Mop, a fluffy cockapoo,
became daffy and incontinent,
but it still took my wife months to convince me
that her "quality of life" was nil,
as ours was becoming.
Next, Mop's daughter, Runt, declined unexpectedly,
The vet wanted $900 just to prop her up,
and could not promise immortality.
So then we were down to one dog,
Ernie, a dachshund left behind by our daughter
when she left us behind.
I called him "the rotund rodent"
and he endured such insults,
believing he was the survivor
who was going to outlive me,
but he didn't.
And then I adopted his successor,
Ralph, also a dachshund, from a rescue shelter,
also, like me, irritable and mortal.
I did him no favor by keeping him alive
after his mind went
and he staggered around the house
like I now sometimes do.

"Mortal Dogs" was originally published in *Our Last Walk: Using Poetry
for Remembering and Grieving Our Pets* by Louis Hoffman, Michael
Moats, and Tom Greening. Reprinted with permission.

Warding Off Death

With enough books, journals, magazines
poems, photographs, recordings, and correspondence
I can ward off death.
Or so I thought.
They are stacked up in two offices.
Winnowing out the ones I really want
is a tedious and ultimately
impossible task.
I will leave their fate to my survivors
who will be more ruthless than I.
The city dump will inherit most of it.
Even the rats there will have to struggle
to keep from being buried.

I'm in Everyone

I am the child who yearns to grow,
the peasant with scarce seeds to sow,
the veteran who walks with pain,
the carpenter who carved his cane.
I am the mom who sits at night,
and prays her child will be all right.
I am the dad whose youth is gone,
who takes his son to greet the dawn,
the criminal who seeks God's grace,
the astronaut in outer space,
the traveler trekking in foreign lands,
the pilgrim lost in desert sands,
the miner digging deep for coal,
the chanteuse singing from her soul,
the skier schussing powder snow,
the farmer digging with his hoe,
the dancer vamping on the stage,
the artist painting joy and rage,
those craving peace, those waging war.
I'm all of these and millions more.
Do not stand at my grave and cry.
I am not there, I did not die.
I am everywhere beneath the sun,
I'm in everything and everyone.

On We Tramp

So on we tramp, close to the end,
less lonely going with a friend
whose soul still beams much needed light
into the fast encroaching night.
If there are rocks strewn on our path,
if nature hurls its baleful wrath
against the two of us today
together we will find our way,
and though this world is harsh, severe,
let's hope some better one is near.

No Fun

At 81 I'd just begun
to make a try at having fun,
but when I reached age 83
I'd learned that fun is not for me.
Instead I'm making lots of room
for dark forebodings and for gloom.
I find this is what I do best
and so I'm on a holy quest
to magnify my suffering,
extort from you more pitying.

Man vs. Tree

This happens every year:
As the sun moves daily across the winter sky
it brightens my gloomy mood
only briefly, and then
disappears behind a giant redwood.
I'd like to cut that tree down
but don't,
though it is on my property
and I have a right.
People, especially frail, old and chilled ones,
should be granted more compassion than trees.
I assert this
but don't know who would understand
if I wielded my chain saw.
So again that giant opaque tree
with its many branches and thick bark
defies me.

Transiency

I'm aging fast and wonder why
we fragile mortals tend to die.
I'm glad I've lived but am perplexed,
and frankly by this plight quite vexed.
But I should ask, why did God give
me precious years in which to live?
I'd like to claim I used them well,
and not on querulous questions dwell.
Still, I don't like this transiency,
and hope it won't apply to me.

Maple Syrup

My California Christmas almost over,
I need consolation,
but humbly settle for a big spoonful
of maple syrup
bottled near your Vermont lakeside house.
Its rich taste brings back my memory
of a visit to you one fall
when you were making syrup from messy sap,
boiling it in a huge kettle
and skimming off impurities.
That was many years ago,
and now we are both seeking
some final sweetness
free of all the stuff that gets mixed in.
Let me know if you find a way
to make it last, even if just
for one more winter.

Stopping

For years I jogged each morning
to the end of my street and back
accompanied by my dog Demian
until one March morning
he stood still and did not follow me.
I called him. No response.
I ran a few feet, stopped, and called him again.
He turned around and slowly walked back to my house.
That morning marked the end of my youth.
Thirty years later Demian is long dead
and I have stopped jogging.
Now I know how he felt
as he stood there
watching me go on with life
without him.

"Stopping" was originally published in *Our Last Walk: Using Poetry for Remembering and Grieving Our Pets* by Louis Hoffman, Michael Moats, and Tom Greening. Reprinted with permission.

Burn my Poems

Some day the poem I write will be my last.
My final writing days will then have passed.
Don't worry–I am sure I'll feel no grief.
Instead, I'll gladly welcome the relief.
My readers, too, will gratefully be free,
not live in dread of further poems from me.
The ones I've written? Throw them in the fire.
I know that they will make a blazing fire.
Thus warmth can come from tepid poetry
and luke-warm verse dispel frigidity.

Still Here

I really hope the end of my career
is decades hence, and certainly not near.
There's so much more I feel obliged to say,
so many problems I must solve some way.
The world depends on my continued care,
and for this reason I would never dare
to leave it in its present sorry state
subject to internecine scorn and hate.
So here I am, and I'll be here a while,
and when I go, I will go out in style.

Is There a Seer?

Is there a seer, one who knows
how I at last can find repose?
I hope someday a healing balm
will ease me into peace and calm,
but so far I have searched in vain
and limp along in dread and pain.
I trust fresh spring will come again
and pray that it will make me sane,
yet can you tell what lies ahead,
if I'll find peace before I'm dead?

Old Dachshund

You know a dog is getting old and desperate
when he starts making up outlandish lies
that even he knows
you won't believe,
like the one my dachshund told me this morning
about how not one but two big coyotes
came in though the small dog door
and peed in my kitchen.
I just looked at him
and he knew his story wasn't working,
but dachshunds are stubborn
and he stuck to it.
So I got the mop and cleaned up
and scowled at him,
and he defiantly scowled back.

"Old Dachshund" was original published in *Our Last Walk: Using Poetry for Remembering and Grieving Our Pets* by Louis Hoffman, Michael Moats, and Tom Greening. Reprinted with permission.

Not Aged

I'll fast become irate and rabid
if you refer to me as "aged."
I'll rant and rave and fiercely pout
if you suggest I might have gout.
I'm healthy, young, in my own mind–
just look at me and you will find
no evidence that I've declined.
Instead, I'm often wined and dined.
So urge me on as I dodge death–
unless you are too out of breath.
The years go by and I'm still here.
I think that I deserve a cheer.

Carry On

Now I'm just an aging wretch
limping down a bleak homestretch
with legs that ache and two sore feet
ready to concede defeat.
Still the autumn grass grows green
thus redeeming this bleak scene.
One more round and then I'm through–
from now on it's up to you.
Carry on as best you can,
even with ersatz elan.

Brain Fade

The fates are playing tricks on me
and tarnishing my brilliancy.
Alas, I have become afraid–
my brain has now begun to fade.
I search for words, for clever rhymes
that graced my verse in better times.
Instead of flaunting fluency
I'm warding off senility.
So be it if the gods decree it.
I'm sad that I am forced to see it.

My Next Incarnation

Surrounded by swarming samsara,
I resist, protest,
try to fight through it,
get entangled,
curse the absent gods,
resign with a petulant but timid growl
which scares no one.
I will plan my next incarnation
more carefully,
making sure it does not include
excursions through mind fields.

Fight Death

Now hear me as I must protest
a noxious fact that I detest:
I've learned that someday I will die,
but was not told the reason why.
I plan to fight this destiny
with all the strength that's left in me.
It clearly is quite undeserved
and it has got me quite unnerved.
Please join me in this righteous fight
to save what is our basic right.

Haunting Question

I like pretending I've no fear of death
and will defy it 'til my dying breath.
I march around as if I'm young and strong,
assured of living healthily and long.
But really I know I'll run out of time,
and after that won't write another rhyme.
While I am here, still vital and alive,
our fragile fumbling species will survive,
but when I'm gone what will survivors do?
I'm sure this is a question haunting you.

Bring Some Sense

Grasping, clutching, craving meaning,
in its absence howling, keening,
here we pace like some crazed beast
mourning for a world that ceased.
Bring fresh sense into our life,
peace instead of mindless strife.
Give us some new raison d'etre
quench the raging storms of hate, or
show a path for our redemption,
from this hell— a circumvention.

To Live Forever

I've reached the ancient age of 85
and there is evidence I'm still alive.
I sleep and eat and often try to breathe,
and search and search for new ways to deceive
myself that I will surely live forever,
for that's become my main long term endeavor.
Each day so far I've managed to endure
has made me ever more convinced and sure
that in the future not too long from now
I'll conquer death, and then I'll show you how.

Master and Pet

My dog insists that I make no mistake:
He barks and barks so I'll know he's awake.
I wish instead he'd let me sleep 'til noon
and not demand that I get up so soon.
He will not let me linger long in bed,
declaring that he should be promptly fed.
I try my best to fulfill his demands,
to quickly do whatever he commands,
but who is pet and who is master here?
I'm sad to say that is no longer clear.

How to Become Real?

I'm much upset and bothered with
the fear that I am just a myth.
I thought God offered me a deal
that somehow I would be quite real.
He let me down, and all I get
is fantasy, and thus I fret,
and fumble, frown, and fulminate,
which hardly helps my angst abate.
Perhaps with Satan I can deal–
What must I do to become real?

How to Keep Young

How to keep young, spry and vital?
Practice adamant denial.
Some get older day by day–
I refuse to live that way.
Yesterday I felt quite young
'til my clavicle got sprung.
Whiskey fixed that right away
and I had a blissful day.
Time may pass but let's deny it.
Aging looms, but I defy it.

Befuddlement

I used to be quite competent,
but now I face befuddlement.
My mind was once a willing slave,
but now it tends to misbehave.
It fumbles, staggers, "drops the ball,"
and I can't count on it at all.
I wish that it again would be
a source of great sagacity.
If it keeps acting like a fool
I'll have to send it back to school.

Not a Crank?

I'm not one of those tiresome cranks?
I happily proffer my thanks!
I do not welcome growing old–
I'd rather strut, pretend I'm bold,
but underneath I quiver, quake,
a covert coward, nerd, and flake.
Please don't tell others I'm this way–
I'd like to fool them one more day.
Alas, my time is running out
and soon all I will do is pout.

Assure Me

I love my life, don't want to leave,
and yet I have begun to grieve.
Time's running out, the months slip by,
I've faced the fact that I will die.
Few years are left–what will I do?
For wise advice I turn to you.
Perhaps you'll give a needed shove
to launch me in a search for love,
or pat me gently on the head,
assure me that I'm not yet dead.

To Any Length

I don't feel very mobile, agile.
Instead I wobble– fragile, docile.
Every move is an endeavor,
but I plan to live forever.
From whence will I get the strength?
I will go to any length:
Drugs, concoctions, incantations,
offering the gods oblations,
trips to far flung mountain nations,
LSD hallucinations....
If you'll ease my dire frustration
you will earn my adulation.

Don't Laugh

I'll spend today warding off
awareness of my mortality.
The day must not end
until I announce I am ready.
I'll write one more poem,
pet the dog,
protest this "reality."
Even then I may need more time
and will loudly demand it,
confident that some greater power
is listening, and cares,
and does not just laugh.

Outwit Death

Old age and death? That's not for me.
I plan to live eternally.
You mortal beings may run out
of time and health, and then may doubt
that I have the capacity
to outwit death and thus be free.
I'll give you lessons if you want
so that unwanted fate won't haunt
you in your precious sunset years
and you'll transcend this vale of tears.

Not Tottering

I won't admit I'm tottering,
dissociative or doddering.
I'm agile, nimble, and alert,
thus my feelings do get hurt
when you treat me as a fool,
claim I'm stubborn as a mule.
My IQ is as high as ever
and I am proud I hardly ever
lose my car keys or my mind,
which I in a few days find.

Late Life Lunacy

I've not found rationality
can cure my late life lunacy,
but let us hope this fact will free me
henceforth to be more blissful, dreamy.
Just still you mind and come with me
into my febrile fantasy.
The world is mad and so are we–
accept this as our destiny.
Such is we mortal's endless curse–
be grateful that our lives aren't worse.

One Last Chance

I hoped that I might end with style and grace,
not with this awkward, fumbling loss of face.
Forgetful, sloppy, senile and what's more,
I have become a prototypal bore.
The wisdom of old age eluded me,
my ego feeds my vacuous vanity.
I moralize, pronounce, pontificate–
I am the elder children love to hate.
In spite of that, before my time must pass,
please give me one last chance to show some class.

Fulfilled

Much to my constant consternation
I'm trapped in this crass incarnation.
Each day brings some humiliation,
a troubling, turgid, perturbation.
I plead this torment soon be ended–
It is not one to be transcended.
But if I'm stuck in this sad tale
with luck I hope I can prevail,
emerge reborn, at last redeemed,
fulfilled more than I ever dreamed.

New Year's Eve with Dog

I do not think I can conceive
of a more boring New Year's Eve.
The dog's not given any sign
he'll sing a cheerful "Auld Lang Syne."
Another home-bound year has passed–
I hope that it won't be my last.
I'm growing old and soon will die
without a visit to Shanghai,
nor have I ever set foot in
that grand Germanic Stadt Berlin.
Because my travels have been narrow
I've never seen Rio Janeiro.
The dog and I, a house-bound pair,
don't plan to travel anywhere.
So here we sit, just he and I,
as one more fleeting year goes by.

Afterlife?

Excuse me, but I must ask why
you claim that someday I will die.
I do not welcome such grim news
and I am seeking other views.
Perhaps there is an afterlife
more peaceful and less torn by strife.
In any case, I must demand
eternal bliss, transcendence, and
a place in heaven guaranteed
before I am from this realm freed.

Addicted to Life

I can't kick this habit
of preserving my life.
I've had it too long.
I should have quit years ago
when I still could have tried other ventures
like martyrdom, self-sacrifice,
fatal heroism or dramatic suicide.
Now I go on and on
repeating myself, boring friends,
spending my childrens' inheritance,
assuring my dog that
I will always be here for him.
The Neptune Society got some money from me
and I got an urn for my ashes,
but it sits there empty
year after year.

Walking Slowly

I walk slowly, carefully, hesitantly,
like an old man.
I don't really need to–
I'm actually agile and spry.
You believe me, and
I thank you for that.
The crutch in my closet?
It's from years ago
when I hurt my leg schussing.
That is no longer a problem
since I gave up skiing.
And I have quit skating
because I tired of going in a circle,
bombarded by bad music.
So if you walk with me
I'll thank you for your patience
and for not noticing
how long it takes to get anywhere,
and for not knowing
where it is worth going.

The Past

So much of value I will leave behind.
Please salvage it, enjoy it,
put it to good use
or not. Who cares?
The past is past: Let it go,
forget it!
No! Grasp it, clutch it
so the present can be evaded
and the future postponed.
But life sputters, stalls,
gears grind, strip.
Where is a mechanic capable
of making this contraption work right
and move forward?

Aging

In life I've turned another page.
This chapter's called "Advancing Age."
I used to wake up feeling fine
but now I feel my slow decline.
My legs are stiff, my back is sore–
I never felt this way before.
The days zoom by, my end is near.
I hear the message loud and clear,
but do not want to face the truth:
I've used up my eternal youth.

Evasion

Some days I feel I'm in the gutter
doomed to pitifully mutter
protests 'gainst my unfair fate,
scared that it is getting late
for my much delayed redemption,
or at least some compensation
for the cruelties I've suffered,
never by God's blessing buffered.
But then with joy I realize
I've still evaded my demise.

Lizard

Please reassure me
that the small nervous lizard on my patio
is not a baby dinosaur
who will grow large, become
a fierce monster,
and take revenge against me
for turning the hose on him
and flushing him away like trash.
Fate will do that to all of us–
you cannot swim against it.
The lizard and I will end up
someplace we did not intend to be,
soaked, confused.

Resist Change

They tell me joys are seldom lasting
but I'm obsessed with firmly grasping
those still within my greedy reach
and will not let experience teach
me how I might move on, be free
to savor life spontaneously.
All change I stubbornly resist,
demanding that the past persist.
Please join me in this great campaign
to rid the world of flux and pain.

An Inspiration?

Some say I am an inspiration.
They must be sunk in desperation.
How can they glean some hope from me?
a lost soul drowned in misery?
Each day I greet the rising sun
still praying life's game can be won.
I struggle on, the years fly by,
and I don't know the reason why.
I dare not total up the score
and fear the stakes we're playing for.

Worth Doing?

When I comfort my beseeching dog
does the world become infinitesimally
more livable?
We will never know,
but the dog claims to know,
and he tells me
it is worth doing.
Perhaps there is a camel in Egypt
who is grateful for something.
I hope he tells others.
Is it too much to ask
for some kind of contagion effect?

Delaying Death

I'm not prepared for growing old–
as I near death I am not bold–
so I've decided to delay
that dreary chore 'till Saturday,
or maybe later on next week,
or maybe I will simply seek
a way to put it off forever....
now there's a challenging endeavor!
I hope that you will help me out
and not stir up in me some doubt.

Anti-Aging

My classmates' children are retiring–
I do not find that fact inspiring.
I can't believe I am that old
in spite of what I have been told.
Just yesterday we graduated,
then some reunions celebrated.
My gait's not slow, my hair's not grey–
at least it wasn't yesterday.
But years keep rushing quickly by–
I fear that someday I might die.

Fighting Aging

No longer confident and bold,
to my dismay I'm growing old.
My dignity is fast eroding,
I shudder with a grim foreboding.
Increasingly confused and stumbling,
I am not lithe–instead I'm fumbling.
Pontificating through my dribbling,
unconscious that I'm heard as quibbling,
I do not age with dignity
but fight it off frenetically.

Burden

My sick and aged mother told me
she didn't want to be a burden,
and now I don't either.
But she was, and I am.
Joy, even contentment,
get squeezed out
by the humiliations of failing embodiment,
the mundane logistics and hassles of care.
How to rise above mere enduring
to celebrate what was...and what is left?

Still Seeking

For my short life I now must grieve.
I really do not want to leave.
It is the only one I've known,
but far too many years have flown.
The sun is setting, night looms near,
my raison d'etre is not clear.
I'm stranded on a rocky shoal,
huge salty waves erode my soul
while still I seek some solace, calm,
an undeserved consoling balm
from heaven or from any place
that can dispense a bit of grace.
Time's running out, I flail and rant.
Survive this storm? Don't say I can't.

Aging with My Dog

As through these final years I slog
I'm grateful for my loving dog.
While I bemoan all that I'm losing
he snuggles and then goes on snoozing.
Each time I start to rant and rave
he says I should my life force save.
From whence does he such wisdom glean
to brighten up my dreary scene?
Is there a god-like dog somewhere
who taught my dog to show such care?

We Will See

Though growing old I will persist
in claiming that I do exist.
The evidence, I must admit,
is disappearing bit by bit,
but I still prance and strut about
in hopes of countering all doubt.
The years have been quite kind to me
in spite of my debauchery,
but that won't last, and we will see
if I can stage a grand finis.

About the Author

Tom Greening earned a B.A. from Yale University, spent a year in Vienna on a Fulbright Fellowship, and attended graduate school at the University of Michigan, earning a PhD in 1958. He is Professor Emeritus from Saybrook University, Clinical Professor of Psychology at the University of California, Los Angeles (UCLA), past Editor of the *Journal of Humanistic Psychology*, and a poet. His mentors included Abraham Maslow, Carl Rogers, Jim Bugental, and Rollo May. He has been in private practice since 1958. Dr. Greening has numerous other books and publications including *Words Against the Void*; *Our Last Walk: Using Poetry for Grieving and Remembering our Pets* (with Louis Hoffman and Michael Moats); *Nasreddin the Psychologist*, a book of droll stories about a wise fool; and *Animals I Have Known*.

.